Happy About® Apartment Management

30 Years of Expert Tips and Advice on Multifamily Property Management

By:
Robert W. Klag, CPA
M. Gary Wong
Steven M. McDonald, CPM®
Gemma G. Lim

HappyAbout.info

21265 Stevens Creek Blvd.
Suite 205
Cupertino, CA 95014

Happy About Apartment Management: 30 Years of Expert Tips and Advice on Multifamily Property Management

First Printing: November, 2006
ISBN 160005031X
Place of Publication: Silicon Valley, California, USA
Library of Congress Control Number: 2006938452

Trademarks

All terms mentioned in this book that are known to be trademarks or service marks have been appropriately capitalized. Westlake Realty Group, Inc. and Happy About® cannot attest to the accuracy of this information. Use of a term in this book should not be regarded as affecting the validity of any trademark or service mark.

Warning and Disclaimer

Every effort has been made to make this book as complete and as accurate as possible, but no warranty of fitness is implied. The information provided is on an "as is" basis. The authors and the publisher shall have neither liability nor responsibility to any person or entity with respect to any loss or damages arising from the information contained in this book.

Praise for 'Happy About Apartment Management'

"Westlake Realty Group is a property management company that understands the owner's perspective, that is, maximizing value and minimizing liabilities and expenses. Westlake not only 'gets it' but equally important, also they get it done. Their advice is invaluable."
Victor B. MacFarlane, Managing Principal, MacFarlane Partners

"Westlake's book provides the reader with a comprehensive treatment of property management. More than simply a collection of forms, the text is a business guide to dealing with the common problems of managing a multi-family rental property. A must read, especially if the property is owned by a trust and you are the trustee."
Bruce F. Anderson, Chairman, First Republic Trust Company

"I have worked with Westlake for over 12 years on various real estate matters. I found them to be extremely competent, knowledgeable and easy to work with. I would not hesitate to recommend them."
Ed Lok, Managing Director, Citigroup Private Bank

"I have had the opportunity to read 'Happy About Apartment Management' and found that is well written and easy to understand. It takes the reader from technology and how it can change aspects of the way in which property managers do their business to the basic 'nuts and bolts' in creating a community with the residence. It sets out a template for screening, collections, and the necessary forms required to manage an apartment complex. A great reference guide. "
William Perry, Vice President - Regional Director
First American Title Insurance Company

ACKNOWLEDGMENT & DEDICATION

This book shares 30 years of knowledge, experience, and great stories by the management and staff of Westlake Realty Group, Inc. We dedicate this book to our founder, T.M. Chang, whose tireless energy has inspired us all.

CONTENTS

PART VII: PORTFOLIO PERFORMANCE

PREFACE

Dear Real Estate Investor:

Most of us have seen infomercials about achieving financial independence by investing in real estate. During my years in property management, I have seen many people build wealth by investing in real estate. I have also seen time forgive some very poor real estate investments, because fortunately, most bad real estate decisions are forgiven as property values appreciate. So, from my perspective, the key attribute to successful real estate investing is longevity—surviving the period between purchase and sale, while the property works to pay its way.

During the appreciation years, many real estate investors realize how poorly prepared they are to manage property. They experience the enormous stress from evictions because they have not developed appropriate credit-screening techniques that identify potential deadbeats. They are sued for discrimination because they do not understand Fair Housing regulations. They fall victim to downward economic spirals because they do not understand the relationship between curb appeal, occupancy rates, and rent. Worst of all, they often don't realize that their properties are underperforming by thousands of dollars each month.

I have always found it illogical that investors pay substantial fees to their stockbrokers yet trust themselves to manage an investment property that is constantly at risk from fire, vandalism, and personal liability lawsuits. Real estate investment can be your path to financial independence if you are willing to give it the attention it requires. All too often, however, investors are ill prepared or unwilling to do so. If you are thinking of managing multiple properties or properties with multiple units, please read this book. Westlake Realty Group has successfully managed real estate for over 30 years. So we think you'll find it a helpful and informative introduction to the fundamentals—and complexities—of property management.

Sincerely,

Robert W. Klag

Robert W. Klag
Chief Executive Officer
Westlake Realty Group, Inc.

WHY WE WROTE THIS BOOK?

REAL ESTATE can be a smart, lucrative investment, because it shelters property appreciation from taxes while allowing owners to deduct interest and depreciation. In addition, unlike financial investments, tax-deferred exchanges are common real estate transactions. However, many investors ignore real estate because it requires daily management. Still others invest in real estate and attempt to manage their properties themselves to save on management fees.

We at Westlake wrote this book because we believe that professional property management makes real estate investment accessible to all investors, just as portfolio management has opened the financial markets to the general population. For those readers who would pay a portfolio manager but are unwilling to use a property manager, we have the following true story:

Susan Hamsher was in pain during our meeting. The owner of two 80-unit apartment buildings located 20 miles apart, she was considering hiring a professional management company. We had visited one of her properties, Cedar Meadows, and had found it in poor condition. Our report noted problems such as abandoned mattresses in carports, exposed nails on a low hanging wooden beam, and a notice that violated Fair Housing rules. Posing as a potential renter, our general manager had made an appointment with the resident manager but upon arrival had found a "post-it" on the office door saying that the manager was picking up someone at the airport. The situation was unfortunate, because Cedar Meadows—with its great location and spacious floor plans—should be giving Susan a good return on her investment.

Susan told us that because her time was spent on managing the two properties, she had missed opportunities to expand and broaden her real estate portfolio. We knew the Westlake team could transform Cedar Meadows into a secure and thriving community so we developed an attractive proposal. Unfortunately, we never heard back from her. Susan is still managing Cedar Meadows. Or, more likely, Cedar Meadows is managing her.

We wrote this book to educate property owners about the complexity of property management and the value-add that the right management team can offer. We understand that relinquishing the day-to-day management role is a challenge for some owners, but our three decades of experience show that property value increases significantly when a professional team is involved.

We believe that the cost savings and increased revenues we achieve through the way we deliver our services , our efficiency, our knowledge of legal compliance issues, and our astute capital improvement programs more than enable us to "pay our way."

TECHNOLOGY & PROPERTY MANAGEMENT

4

PART II: TECHNOLOGY AND PROPERTY MANAGEMENT

CHAPTER 1

TECHNOLOGY: THE FUTURE OF PROPERTY MANAGEMENT

echnology is rapidly transforming property management. Because he most effective technologies are typically PC and Internet based, hey are available to all property management companies. Equally nportant is a manager's ability to seamlessly incorporate technoloy into existing operations. The most progressive and dynamic orgaizations in the industry will lead the way, leaving behind those with ess foresight.

Westlake supports proven management expertise with the practial application of state-of-the art technology, differentiating ourselves om competitors by the way we deliver our services. We believe that our mployees can be more efficient and productive than the norm, because e equip them with tools that enable them to conduct business whether hey are in their offices or on the road.

OLLOWING ARE A FEW EXAMPLES OF THE WAY TECHNOLOGY HAS ENHANCED OUR OPERATIONS:

MAGE TECHNOLOGY

ssentially, Westlake's "file cabnet" is our network server. Regardless of physical locaion, an employee can access the nformation on our secure central latabase. And with image techology, anyone with a PC and the ppropriate level of permission an access the same information imultaneously — saving time and ncreasing productivity. Image echnology eliminates the possibility of losing or misplacing files, allows us to track who has viewed a document, and enables us to see the changes they have made.

Our invoice approval process, for example, is an intelligent application of image technology. We scan invoices, route them electronically to each approving manager, and electronically record each step in the approval process. Approvals, which are based on a pre-determined spending authorization limit, must be recorded before a check can be issued. The invoice payment process is secure, quick, and efficient, and it provides anytime, anywhere management access.

GPS TECHNOLOGY (GLOBAL POSITIONING SYSTEM)

Property management is a service industry, and people are our most critical resource. To increase productivity, we equip our staff with GPS phones linked to Internet-based software that "knows" where they are. An integrated work-order system "knows" what they are doing throughout the work day. Ask yourself: "Does your property manager know where maintenance staff was on Thursday at 11 o'clock?" With GPS, Westlake property managers know where staff is working and can clock assignments by work order.

ELECTRONIC BANKING

Westlake is a leader in implementing new banking processes. For years, we have offered our tenants effortless rent payment through an automated clearing house (ACH)—meaning that tenants do not have to remember to pay rent or worry about late fees. The ACH also enables property managers to collect rents without processing checks for deposit. For those residents who insist on paying their rent by check, Internet deposits through Check 21 is the latest banking efficiency, allowing property managers to scan and deposit rent checks electronically without going to the bank. Corporate staff has immediate access to deposits as well as the ability to view front and back images of individual checks.

PROPERTY OWNER OVERSIGHT

Technology facilitates an owner's visibility into operations and enhances the property manager–owner relationship. Simply by entering a web-based portal, an owner can participate at any stage of the management process. Currently, most property management companies do not offer this capability, but over time it will become the industry benchmark. Will your current property manager be able to respond effectively as your real estate portfolio expands?

Innovatively-applied technology can reduce the burden of administrative duties, making it possible for managers to focus more intensively on properties and their tenants. Companies with the insight and ability to smoothly integrate technology into existing operations will save the property owners they serve significant time and expense.

8 BASIC QUESTIONS TO ASK YOURSELF

CHAPTER 2

In the first chapter, we discussed the benefits technology provides to property management operations. In this chapter, we turn to a more fundamental topic: the decision to hire property management expertise vs. doing it yourself.

Most owners find that managing their properties are what they expected. If you decide to manage your own property, think through what's involved in managing it effectively and profitably. The following eight questions will help you in that process:

1 Can you commit to being on call?

As property manager, you can expect calls at any time of day or night. Your tenants will call you personally and expect you to resolve problems or sort out disputes immediately. If you've hired staff, you will have to deal with the personnel management issues, like the sudden departure of a key employee.

Can you commit to dropping whatever you're doing and focusing on property management issues?

2 Do you have time to make many small decisions?

You are responsible for the results of all decisions made by on-site resident managers. You must decide:

- How much spending authority will you grant them?
- Will they make leasing decisions?
- Will they make collection and eviction decisions?
- Can you entrust them to select vendors objectively?

Consider the cost of a poorly handled eviction or the problems created by unscrupulous vendors. The one sure way to avoid poor staff decision making or outright fraud is to make the decisions yourself. Is that what you want?

3 Can you visit your property frequently?

You should plan on walking your property a couple of times a week, including nights and weekends. The U.S. courts use a standard of "knew or should have known" to judge negligence. That means you will be held liable for unsafe conditions on your property even if you didn't know they existed.

4 Do you want to see your name in the local paper?

Whenever there is news regarding your property, you are considered the public spokesperson. While you can set up a legal structure that insulates you from some personal liabilities, you won't be able to avoid publicity. As owner / manager, expect residents to mention you by name to reporters.

5 Can you make time for property management seminars?

Laws affecting rental properties change constantly. As property manager, it is your job to keep up with all the changes. If seminars are your thing, you are in luck. You'll have your choice of many seminars—usually scheduled on Saturdays or evenings.

6 Do you want to represent yourself in court?

Seminars alone will not keep you out of court. Residential property management is highly regulated. Many statutes and legal entities exist solely to resolve disputes between landlords and tenants. As property manager, you will need to learn this complex and constantly changing system quickly.

7 Are you really looking for a second job?

When you buy and manage your own property, you are taking on a second job. Was that your intention when you invested in income property? Is property management the highest and best use of your time? Would you be better off investing that time in building your property portfolio and focusing on your primary profession or business? How well does property management pay if, after taxes, you keep only half of what you save in management fees?

8 Why do you own property?

Is income property a smart investment if managing it turns into a second job? Hiring a property management company is no different than hiring a financial advisor. A reputable firm offers the expertise, screening procedures, and rent-collection policies that increase your peace of mind and cash flow. With the management of your property investment in good hands, you have more time to focus on creating wealth by increasing your portfolio of real estate properties.

OCCUPANCY & MARKETING

10 WAYS TO MAINTAIN OCCUPANCY IN A BUYER'S MARKET

CHAPTER 3

Every landlord competes with tenants' desires for home ownership. However, retaining tenants for the long haul is possible if you encourage the right mindset.

1 It's about living the good life

Where and how we live is deeply connected to who we are. The more opportunities you offer residents to control their environment, the less likely they are to move. Combine a desirable lifestyle with freedom from the ongoing care and maintenance of a home, and you set the gold standard for the residents of your community.

For example, allow tenants to personalize their surroundings. Some renters want to "escape" those deadly off-white apartment walls to purchase homes—so why not offer a choice of wall color? Henry Ford advertised that customers could have any color they wanted as long as it was black, and in the process, kept his costs down. If cost control alone is your strategy, it will fail you as it did Ford when Chevrolet offered a range of colors for a few dollars more.

2 Sell the benefits

Providing meaningful benefits supports your tenants' interests on an emotional level and engages with them personally. People are drawn to benefits. There is a difference between a benefit and a feature. "752 square feet of living space" is a feature. A shorter commute is a benefit. A swimming pool is a feature. Having the extra time to swim is a benefit. Help prospective tenants visualize benefits and they will "move in" before they even hire the mover.

Here's an example of creating an emotional connection: "Anne, you mentioned you love to run, but you've been getting home so late that you haven't been able to exercise regularly. If you lived here, your commute would be shorter, and you would have more time to run. Which is a better lifestyle for you?"

3 Promote lifestyle concepts

Sell the "resort" aspects of renting. Renters benefit from better locations, better amenities, better service, less housework, and more free time. Compared to buying, the costs and risks of renting are far lower. Make it clear to your tenants that the benefits of renting far outweigh the inconveniences of home ownership.

4 Remind prospects of the trade-offs

Help them picture hours spent commuting or working on home maintenance vs. time spent with family, convenient shopping, recreational amenities, and other appealing benefits. Present renting not as a lifestyle compromise but a conscious choice for a better life.

5 Point out the positives: Exploit your market strength

Remember, renters must often buy their first homes an hour or more from where they work. Typically, more affordable homes are located in areas without adequate public infrastructure. New developments and suburbs simply haven't had the time to develop good school systems, roads, shopping areas, and other advantages that people who live in established areas take for granted. Make sure your staff knows how to sell the advantages of your location to potential residents.

6 Create a community residents can call home

What are your strengths? Why do people enjoy living in your property? What keeps current residents from moving? You need to "find and remind." Lead with your strengths. Mention them in your brochures and on your website. Include them in your close.

Humans are social beings. We all need and long to feel connected with others. Your residents should feel an attachment to and within their community.

Take advantage of people's desire to belong. Offer activities and events that strengthen relationships and allow residents to make new friends. Welcome newcomers with a gift basket or personal note. A community is more than just mere housing, and a sense of community is what makes renters feel they have found a home.

7 Differentiate your property from the competition

The more your property feels like a community, the more difficult it will be for residents to think about leaving. You can provide the following eight quick but effective community services at little or no cost:

- Morning coffee in the clubhouse. This is a great opportunity to greet your residents every day.
- Much-needed but easily overlooked items for sale. Your ability to come to residents' aid or save them an unwanted trip to the store will endear you to

them. Consider offering tape, band-aids, blank cards, snacks, or other helpful items for sale.

- Stamps and shipping labels. Residents will appreciate your help in sending out important packages, especially during the holidays. Get bonus points by offering to have the rental office hold packages for pickup.
- A community guide. This is an invaluable resource, but residents must know where to find it. Mention it when a lease is signed and advertise it on posters in public areas. Better yet, welcome residents with it the day they move in.
- Laundry and dry cleaning drop-off and pickup. Nobody wants to wait in the rental office for laundry and dry cleaning to arrive. Leave voice mail messages to tell residents when laundry or drycleaning is ready to pickup.

  Regular periodicals in the clubhouse. Residents will love leafing through magazines without having to worry about accumulating piles of back issues. Instead of subscribing to different magazines for your community, you might consider asking residents to contribute their own gently-used magazines to share or trade with others.
- Mass transit schedules and maps. Make them readily available to residents—perhaps in the rental office, clubhouse, or laundry facilities.

8 Evaluate property benefits based on advertising results

If, at the end of a 30-day cycle, an advertised benefit produces no leads, test another potential benefit. The bottom line: your property's best benefits are those that bring in the most qualified traffic. Keep testing until you identify them.

9 Keep your property fresh and appealing with the latest amenities

To maintain your competitive edge, keep lifestyle-oriented amenities up to date. Do your homework to understand the amenities that will be appealing to your community. Resident surveys can be an excellent source of information. So can mystery shopping your competitors' properties.

10 Target non traditional households

Separation and divorce constantly create new family units, and there are now more single-parent than two-parent households. These new family groups are more likely to be renters, and they have different needs than traditional households. Do some research to learn what these potential renters are looking for, and focus your marketing energies there.

I can't believe
the walls match my
bed sheets!

CHAPTER 4

10 WAYS TO KEEP RESIDENTS FROM MOVING

How residents feel about where they live is as important as how they feel about their own apartments. People tend to stay when they feel part of the community. Strengthen the community, and you'll strengthen your residents' desire to remain.

1 Develop a management team who can create emotional bonds with residents

The following "Do's" and "Don'ts" can transform property management into community management:

- Do encourage staff to greet everyone sincerely – by their first names.
- Do keep a fresh pot of coffee ready to encourage residents to visit the office or front desk.
- Do deliver gifts and friendly notes, preferably by hand.
- Do set up a mini-library, magazine collection, or paperback book exchange.
- Do pay attention to convenience. Set up a tool lending service, or make important items like stamps readily available.
- Don't address tenants by their apartment numbers.
- Don't forget to respect a resident's privacy and personal property at all times.
- Don't delay when a tenant requests maintenance or a repair.

2 Publish a regular community newsletter

Newsletters keep everyone informed and connected. Use the newsletter to announce activities that will help create a vibrant community life at your property.

Some ideas for newsletters include:

- Reminding tenants of amenities and benefits they may not have used
- Sharing recipes, special events, or birthdays and graduations
- Including photos of the last community picnic or holiday party.

3 Schedule community activities

Every community is different, so experiment to determine the activities that work best with your residents. Gatherings provide great opportunities for residents to meet and build a genuine sense of community.

Community-building activities you might want to try include:

- Card or bingo games
- A regular Friday night party around the pool
- Children's holiday parties
- Movie night with popcorn and soda
- An informal tennis ladder

Keep events focused on residents and avoid management or owner presentations. Otherwise, you risk turning a celebration into a business event and alienating residents.

You can even invite people from the neighborhood to participate in your community by:

- Offering your property as a polling place
- Letting the Boys Scouts or Girl Scouts meet there
- Hosting a blood drive
- Creating a bulletin board that advertises joint resident/neighborhood activities and services

These ideas will expose your property to the greater community, provide networking opportunities for residents, and lead a stream of prospective residents to your door.

4 Survey residents regularly

Keep your finger on the pulse of resident satisfaction. Include a survey card with all services, repairs, or newsletters. Make survey forms available outside the office, on your website, and in every employee's tool bag, briefcase, or notebook. You need to know the good, the bad, and the ugly about resident perceptions before they start thinking or talking about issues outside your earshot or consider moving.

5 Add a personal touch

Americans are more transient than ever, moving farther and farther from family and friends. A birthday card signed by staff members can solidify the relationship between you and a resident. Write ersonal notes like: "It was good o see you at the pool the other lay! Have a fabulous birthday!" r "I've enclosed a certificate for pplebee's. Have a special birthlay dinner on me." You can make ew residents feel even more welome by giving them a special gift. cts of kindness go a long way.

6 Exceed expectations

ike cars, apartments need reglar maintenance. When mainenance staff members are on ervice calls, have them check to ee if other repairs are required. Is here a leaky faucet, caulking that eeds repair, or furnace filter that hould be replaced? Everyone ppreciates staff that goes the xtra mile.

7 Invest in your on-site team's appearance

ppearance makes the critical first mpression. On-site staff should lways look (and act) like consumnate professionals and be easily dentifiable through uniforms or photo ID tags. Whatever you hoose, a professional appearance gives residents peace of nind and helps them trust your staff.

8 Maintain your property

Curb appeal may bring tenants in, but dirty trash bins and stairways will force them out. If residents are offended by poor maintenance or embarrassed by friends or relatives' comments, they'll consider moving. Fix eyesores like broken fixtures, trash, or graffiti immediately.

Your property is like a hotel, except your guests stay longer and expect much more. Apartment dwellers may not own the real estate, but they do own the lifestyle it affords them. The key to lease renewals is found in your staff's attention to detail.

Regarding maintenance: Nothing is more upsetting to tenants than not being able to talk to someone about a problem. If you track maintenance issues electronically, offer tenants an option for making contact with a human. Provide a face behind the interface.

9 Think renewal

Simply put, residents move because they have developed a bad impression of your property.

Your staff must understand that being "resident-centered" is about attitude—as exemplified by a friendly wave from the gardener, a pleasant greeting from the maintenance supervisor, or a door held open. Keep in mind the image of a five-star hotel—everything must come together for the comfort of the guests.

If residents are happy, they will stay. Work at keeping lines of communication open and understand that every contact with a resident becomes an opportunity to positively influence lease renewal.

10 Ask tenants to stay

Never assume that a resident will renew a lease. Make sure your staff is trained to encourage lease renewals and is familiar with the legal requirements intrinsic to property management.

Send your first request for a lease renewal 60 to 90 days in advance of the deadline and provide an appropriate incentive for responding quickly. Tell residents that you value them with expressions like, "We'd love for you to stay." Or, "You are well-liked in our community. You belong here!!"

When a tenant renews, send a "Welcome Back" gift. Because renewals are less expensive than original leases, this gift should be nicer than the original welcome gift.

CURB APPEAL
FIRST IMPRESSIONS COUNT
CHAPTER 5

Curb appeal is more than a mowed lawn, trimmed hedges, and attractive planting. It's anything that affects how your property is perceived when compared with the competition. Look carefully at the appearance of your property from the street. What you see is critical to your marketing and tenant retention efforts.

Focusing on your property's curb appeal is a business decision with direct and immediate consequences. The actions you take determine who comes, who stays, and what they are willing to pay.

Don't let prospects drive away before they see what you have to offer. This chapter features a cautionary tale about a property with great features, spacious floor plans, and even attached garages—but poor curb appeal.

In newspaper ads, Old Woods Apartments looked great. The property was in a prime location, had top-notch amenities, and was competitively priced. The property was well maintained and in excellent condition. Yet, the leasing staff was convinced that Old Woods could not compete with the Modern Manner Apartments across the street.

During one review, the Old Woods manager told the property owner, "I think our ads actually keep Modern Manner full. I've watched cars pull into our driveway, turn around, and head right across the street straight to their leasing office." Her comments were not far from the truth. Well maintained though it was, Old Woods' looked dated. Its textured-wood facade had not been attractive, so prospective residents could not get past it to consider the property's advantages.

It was not easy to convince the owner to make a substantial investment in new exterior siding and to re-landscape the property, because he did not believe that anything other than lower rents would attract tenants.

However, after re-siding and landscaping, occupancy shot up from a soft 70% to more than 95%+. Occupancy remained strong, supporting substantial rent increases. Ironically, Modern Manor's staff is now complaining that they can't compete with the garages at Old Woods. Of course, Old Woods' owner is now a true believer in the importance of curb appeal.

You may not need to spend thousands of dollars per unit to improve curb appeal, but you do need to view your property from a potential resident's perspective. Ask yourself: "What do prospects see when they first arrive?" If you can't answer that question, ask someone who's never seen the property for feedback and listen carefully to what they say.

Curb appeal starts before someone ever reaches your driveway. Think about the potential routes prospects will travel en route to your property. For example, one 200-unit property sits equidistant between two freeway exits. One exit routes the driver past a stone quarry, the other past a beautiful country club. Which directions do your advertisements provide? Curb appeal is paying attention to the little things.

CLOSING THE SALE

CHAPTER 6

The key to closing a sale is creating a sense of urgency.

A sense of urgency may be directly related to a limited supply. For example, one property management team advertised that it had no units currently available at a new property but that it would be happy to place prospective tenants on a waiting list. The campaign was a huge success because it created a sense of urgency. When openings became available, they inspired swift decisions to rent.

With an existing property, you can develop this sense of urgency by limiting the number of units "available" each day. If you choose this approach, document the specific unit numbers "available" and show these units to every prospect that comes to the property. Providing different information to different potential residents could be construed as a Fair Housing violation. For the same reason, never hold an apartment without a documented deposit.

If a prospect is not willing or able to make a commitment, get their contact information and inform them when a unit becomes available. Again, ensure that your follow-up is consistent for all prospective tenants because of Fair Housing regulations.

PROPERTY MANAGEMENT

APPLICATION

9 KEYS TO CREDIT SCREENING

CHAPTER 7

Your first line of defense against property damage and collection problems is credit screening. Credit screening will save you a lot of grief.

1 Without credit screening, bad risks will find you

Residents who don't pay their rent or break house rules are not randomly distributed across rental communities. Higher concentrations of less desirable applicants inevitably occur in the communities that don't screen well. Make sure you scrutinize your prospects' history.

2 Bad risks waste staff time

The cost of managing and removing delinquent residents is significant, but the cost of eviction is even higher. The most effective, least expensive means of handling resident risk is to screen bad residents out at the beginning of the process.

3 Establish standards

When screening credit, establish a minimum required credit score, and adhere to it. Understand that inconsistencies in this area can appear to be a Fair Housing violation. There are professional shoppers who earn their living finding Fair Housing violations.

4 Do not relax them

When occupancy is down, it is tempting to relax credit screening standards. The temptation is worse when aggressive lease-ups are required. Do not succumb to pressure. Poor risks invariably cost far more in the long run than an apartment left vacant until a qualified resident comes along.

5 Screen prudently

Screen prudently for credit, current employment, income, and rental experience. Keep your focus on the applicant's history and ability to pay rent on time and follow community rules. Follow screening procedures consistently to protect yourself from Fair Housing litigation.

6 Require confirmation

Require a copy of a recent pay stub to confirm employment and ensure net pay is a specific multiple of the monthly rent. The actual percentage varies with the market. The most important point is to establish and adhere to one standard.

7 Obtain unlawful detainer reports

When evaluating a prospect's rental experience, use a reporting service that checks for unlawful detainer actions against the applicant. Confirm that the name on the report exactly matches the name of the applicant. Then verify the name with the evicting attorney or landlord before rejecting the application.

8 Verify identification

The experienced "bad resident" is familiar with how properties screen and often use an alias or proxy. To ensure valid identification, require a government-issued, picture identification card from all applicants. Include every adult living in the apartment in the application and screening process. This will ensure that a proxy applicant is not fronting for a bad prospect.

9 Handle exceptions offsite

Occasionally, someone who does not quite meet standards will ask for an exception. One example of a viable exception is someone who has recently changed jobs. Another example is a resident with adequate credit and income but no previous rental experience.

Do not discuss exceptions with an applicant before accepting and processing an application. Never discuss potential problems or hypothetical situations before taking an application. This invites a Fair Housing complaint. Defer the decision to an off-site management team review, which takes the pressure off your property manager.

CHAPTER 8

4 WAYS TO IMPROVE YOUR COLLECTIONS

The non-payment of rent can often be the start of a confrontational relationship between a resident and management. While staff is primarily interested in collecting rent, residents who are delinquent in paying rent can resort to accusing management of offensive actions, unacceptable conditions, and personal slights. Prevent such problems with the following procedures:

1 Contact the resident quickly and directly when payment is behind schedule

The tenant may have forgotten to write the check. Call and offer to pick it up. Initially, your goal is to distinguish forgetful residents from those who are intentionally not paying you.

2 Preserve your rights by quickly serving legal notices

Be aware of your jurisdiction's legal requirements for unlawful detainer. Do not make the critical error of considering an eviction notice as the end of the process. To evict a tenant, you must follow the law exactly.

3 Get tough

Retain an unlawful detainer attorney. Negotiate a fee structure which includes having the attorney's staff handle all contacts with the resident.

4 Stay tough

Essentially, you want your property to have a reputation for being tough in the area of on-time rent payments. A reputation for laxity attracts bad credit risks. The easier you are on past-due accounts, the more of them you'll have.

Have you never heard of A.C.H?
rent collection

6 REASONS TO USE ACH

CHAPTER 9

Automated Clearing House (ACH) transactions put the rent collection process under your control and avoid the paperwork involved in processing checks and money orders. Including an ACH option with your rental program is a smart idea:

1 ACH reduces your workload

No more filling out deposit slips, copying checks, or closing the office while you go to the bank. ACH transactions save time you can put to more effective use.

2 Late rent payment fees are a thing of the past

Residents automatically make rent payments when they are due.

3 Non-sufficient funds (NSF) problems surface quickly

Most NSF-ACH transactions are reported a day after processing, while checks drawn on insufficient funds can take several weeks to go through the banking system.

4 Rent payments are on time

Rental payments arrive automatically month after month.

5 You have more time for the real matters

Because ACH transactions are automatic, staff has more time to address serious collection problems.

6 ACH eliminates float

ACH eliminates the several days of bank float that is normal with paper checks.

FORMS EVERY LANDLORD SHOULD HAVE

CHAPTER 10

Forms designed for managing apartments can be found on the internet, through professional associations or trade groups, and at stationery stores. The competitive nature of the rental market, plus the legal requirements surrounding property management, has made standardized forms a necessity. Drafting your own without legal review is an invitation to a lawsuit. Following are forms used by any well-run community:

1 Visitor Card

A visitor card is a widely accepted way to gather information from prospects, and it can be used for future follow-up. Many property management software systems integrate the information on visitor cards into application processing to avoid duplication of effort.

2 Application

This form should include everything required to effectively and legally screen applicants. Applications are part of the legal contract binding your prospective resident to your property. Inaccuracies or missing information provide a legal basis for declining the application.

The application form must present a complete picture of the applicant including credit, job, and any legal history; and it must pass legal review for content. The cost of an attorney's review is insignificant considering the importance of this document.

3 Lease Agreement

A lease or rental agreement presents the terms and conditions that bind the owner and the resident. Because of its central importance, the lease must meet all statutory requirements. Landlord/tenant laws are inherently local, so a real estate attorney who is familiar with your location should review your lease agreement (and all other legal documents).

4 Resident Waivers

Discuss these waivers with an attorney and have residents sign them along with the lease agreement. You can obtain resident waivers for acts of nature, third-party actions, actions beyond your (or your agent's) control, and any claim above actual damages for simple negligence.

5 ACH Authorization Form

Because it is desirable (see chapter 9) for as many residents as possible to make ACH rent payments, consider giving them incentives to participate in this program.

6 Move-In Inspection

In any court action, landlords must provide "executed" documentation of the apartment's move-in condition. "Executed" means that the tenant has reviewed and signed off on a checklist of items in the apartment and their condition.

Documentation is crucial in settling damage claims. Before move-in, a staff member must walk through the apartment with the resident and photograph any outstanding problem. After the problem has been resolved, staff should take a second picture. Equally important, the resident should sign the checklist with the manager on the day of move-in. Copies of the sign-offs and photographs must remain in your files.

7 Move-Out Inspection

The move-out form certifies the condition of the property before and after move-out. Before move-out, a staff member should walk through the apartment with the resident. If they disagree about the condition of the property, the staff member should take a photograph. After move-out, a staff member should take pictures of any other damage. It is important to date and file all photos. Thorough documentation is necessary before charging a tenant for property damage.

8 Non-Payment Notice(s)

Every state has different requirements for non-payment notices. Protect yourself from non-paying residents by dealing with them as quickly as the law allows. Have an attorney review your notices and calendar of deliveries.

9 Security Deposit Report

Security deposits must be returned to residents within a statutory period. If a tenant receives less than the full security deposit, the landlord must attach a detailed report of all deductions as well as copies of relevant invoices, and pertinent civil code to the refund check.

10 Repair Request

Some repairs, like those involving plumbing and heat / air conditioning, should be done within a reasonable period. Repairs related to electrical systems or personal safety must be addressed immediately and documented. If you process repair requests electronically, you have documentation that is unassailable in court.

11 Feedback Cards "How are we doing?"

Although not legally required, feedback cards help you know what residents are thinking. Every staff member should carry feedback cards, and extra cards should be available at all property offices. You can provide postage-paid cards or simply ask residents to drop them off at the office.

12 Entry Notices "We've been by"

The law requires that landlords inform residents whenever they have entered their apartment. You can expand this legal requirement into a marketing opportunity.

For residents' safety, track every employee entering an occupied apartment, including the arrival time, purpose, and duration. Create a procedure that warns anyone entering an apartment that a staff member is inside the unit making a repair.

AFFORDABLE HOUSING

SMART WAYS TO RELIEVE SECTION 42 HEADACHES

CHAPTER 11

WHAT IS SECTION 42?

Section 42 projects provide federal Tax Credits to property developments where rent is discounted from market rates to provide "Affordable Housing" to qualified residents. Tax credits are usually syndicated through financial institutions and provide the investment capital for a significant portion of the property construction.

Property owners must follow the Section 42 compliance rules carefully to avoid jeopardizing the status of the tax credits.

1 Invest in a management team that is experienced in managing Tax Credit Properties

With conventional properties, property managers are primarily interested in renting at the highest rate possible and making sure that every resident can pay the rent.

In the case of Tax Credit properties, you must make sure that your management team knows how to qualify residents in compliance with income and rent guidelines. Your team must know the rules and how to document compliance.

2 Invest in staff training

A little training goes a long way. With market rate properties, poor resident screening processes can result in residents who cause problems. With Tax Credit properties, the smallest miscalculation in qualifying residents can result in tax recapture and immediate financial loss to investors.

3 Team with a Tax Credit Specialist

Have your property audited privately before a public audit by the Tax Credit Allocation Committee (TCAC). When the TCAC finds non-compliance, it reports it to the IRS on a form 8823. Work with the appropriate authority in other states. Working with a tax specialist will reduce or prevent the mistakes that lead to the issuance of an 8823 to the IRS.

4 Maintain an up-to-date property fact sheet

Making a current fact sheet available to your staff reduces compliance mistakes. Much of maintaining compliance at a Tax Credit property involves unit type and qualifying the resident's income. By providing staff with a checklist of the property's obligations to the allocation agency, you can avoid most compliance errors.

5 Keep a current development map for mixed-used property

If your property is both affordable and market rate, it can be tricky to stay compliant. Create and maintain a development map that indicates the status of each unit. Unless you do so, the ratio of market-to-subsidized housing can fall out of compliance.

6 Follow the "next available unit" rule for move-ins

Upon move-in, each Tax Credit resident's income must be under a designated cap, and income must be reconfirmed annually. The resident's income must remain under 140% of the income cap. If not, the "next available unit rule" applies. It is essential for property managers to know how to navigate this complex section of the Code.

7 Derive maximum allowable income based on the most current area median income limits

Because rents are capped at percentages of the area median income (adjusted for household size), property managers must be alert to any change and adjust rents accordingly. Check area median income statistics every year.

8 Know the compliance rules for pre-1990 properties

If your property achieved Section 42 status before 1990, rents are based on family size—a calculation that usually produces lower rents than those based on regulations issued in 1990. In 1990, owners were given the option of charging rent based on unit size rather than family size. Unless you elected to charge based on unit size, rent must be based on the actual number of persons in the household.

9 Check utility allowances regularly

Stay current with utility allowances published by the local public housing authority. Because residents are restricted to a maximum combined rent and utilities, rents must be adjusted as utility costs rise and fall. Don't risk noncompliance by overcharging rent. Conversely, don't leave money on the table by undercharging if utility allowances decrease.

ASSET MANAGEMENT

Yesterday, you said you had a leak.

6 REASONS TO **AVOID DEFERRED MAINTENANCE**

CHAPTER 12

Deferring maintenance is an indisputable way to reduce the value of your property. Owners who are interested in maximizing the net operating income (NOI) of their properties will likely be tempted to improve cash flow by putting off seemingly insignificant repairs. Avoid this temptation. Deferring maintenance has long-term negative consequences.

1 Deferred maintenance costs more

Industry studies prove that deferring maintenance costs much more than regular upkeep. Material and labor costs go up. Plumbing and roofing repairs are always more costly because even a small leak can result in extensive water damage, mold problems, or wood rot. It's more difficult and expensive to replace a wall or remove mold than to clean a gutter. The "little things" like uncaulked windows, unrepaired gutters, misdirected sprinklers, and uncleaned drains can do significant structural damage to your property.

2 Rental income suffers

Deferring maintenance creates a downward spiral. The property loses its attractiveness and appeal. It doesn't take long for an "A" property to become an "A-," then "B," and so on. The property becomes harder to lease, and occupancy falls below market average. Rents don't keep pace with the competition, and repairs become more difficult to finance from operating income.

3 Unattractive properties attract unattractive tenants

As the appearance of a property declines, potential residents lose interest in it. You lower screening standards to maintain occupancy. Now you must contend with mounting maintenance costs, reduced income, and a more challenging resident base. The cycle is hard to reverse—making the cost of a regular maintenance program seem quite reasonable.

4 As the cost of capital goes up, a property's collateral value goes down

Options for borrowing for a deferred maintenance property are limited and become significantly more expensive. Institutional lenders decline to make loans or make it difficult. For example, agencies such as Fannie Mae and Freddie Mac require an escrow of 150% of the cost of all deferred maintenance on the property.

The bottom line: If your building has significant deferred maintenance, you will pay more to qualify for a significantly smaller loan.

5 Repairing the damage to your property's reputation is expensive

By the time the quality of your residents has declined, merely making repairs will not improve your property's reputation. For apartment communities, restoring a reputation requires costly property remarketing efforts such as removing undesirable tenants, renaming the property, improving curb appeal, and creating new marketing materials. This complex task is closer to redevelopment than property management. Owners who lack the capacity to turn properties around are forced to sell or trade them at less than true value.

6 Be proactive

If you're not moving ahead, you're falling behind. You must continuously make repairs and replacements and create a long term plan with the proper level of financial allocations. Committing a percentage of the property's gross rent is a commonsense way to make such a plan feasible.

7 WAYS TO IMPROVE YOUR ROI

CHAPTER 13

The most significant increases in Return on Investment (ROI) from real estate are realized through appreciation in property value. In general, a property's valuation is based on its capitalization rate (cap rate). Valuation by cap rate is similar to generating the present value of an annuity where the annuity is the property's net operating income (NOI). Such a calculation would look like this:

$$\text{Estimated Value} = \frac{\text{NOI}}{\text{Cap Rate}}$$

Example: A property has a NOI of $120,000. Cap rates in the area for this type of property average about 12%.

$$\text{Estimated Market Value} = \frac{\$120{,}000}{0.12} = \$1{,}000{,}000$$

NOI is determined by subtracting both the vacancy factor and operating expenses from the property's gross income.

Operating expenses do include advertising, insurance, maintenance, property taxes, property management, repairs, supplies, and utilities. Operating expenses do not include capital improvements, such as a new roof; personal property such as a lawn mower; mortgage payments; income and capital gains taxes; loan origination fees, and similar expenses.

Following are seven suggestions for raising the value of a property by increasing its NOI and cap rate:

1 Increase occupancy

The cap rate model generates value from rented units, so the buyer gets vacant units for free. While this isn't completely true, high occupancy builds high value.

2 Raise rent

Many properties, especially privately-owned ones, charge below-market rents. Under-pricing typically stems from poor property management.

Shop the market. Find three properties that compare to yours. If their rents are higher, consider realigning yours. A $10 per month rent increase on a 100-unit property increases its value by $120,000.

3 Increase fees

Does the application fee at your community cover the real cost of processing an application? What about delinquency and returned check fees? If a property processing five applications a week raises the application fee by $10, the property's overall value would increase by $26,000 with a 10% cap rate.

4 Increase non-rental (ancillary) income

One of the greatest reasons to rent versus purchasing a home is lifestyle convenience. Apartment dwellers are a captive market for life-enhancing on-site services. Charging appropriate fees for specialized services has become the newest source of additional income for many owners.

You may also want to consider contracting affinity programs like health club memberships for your property. They give your community a greater competitive edge and provide additional revenue streams.

5 Reduce expenses but not quality of service

Look for new and more efficient processes to build into your property's purchasing system. For example, would new equipment reduce labor costs?

In property management, every dollar saved is $10 earned. Given the multiplying effect of the cap rate, the financial value of every improved system is multiplied by the number of units on the property.

6 Move up

Grade A properties have lower cap rates and higher property values than A- or B properties and so on throughout the continuum. The higher the grade, the lower the cap rate.

Age, amenities, condition, and services determine the grade of a property. Fortunately, owners can address all these factors. Even age can be reversed with a slight rehabilitation of the exterior and common areas. Perceived age matters and can be influenced positively with a renovation or negatively through deferred maintenance—in turn moving the property's market value up or down.

7 Move over

Different sub-markets often have very different cap rates. Properties on the cusp of two sub-markets must work proactively to be included in the submarket of choice. Such properties maximize value by selecting a sub-market with higher-valued properties.

Attention to every public detail of the property is key. Make sure that primary signage, telephone exchange, marketing focus and even small things such as the directions to your property are targeted to your preferred sub-market.

CHAPTER 14

5 COMMON LAWSUITS LANDLORDS CAN AVOID

Landlords have long been popular targets for litigation. With careful planning, these lawsuits don't have to happen.

1 Condition of the property

Landlords are regularly sued for "slip and fall" incidents, where a resident slips on a "trip hazard" and sues for injuries. Avoid this liability by regularly touring the property, seeking out potential hazards such as uneven walkways and low-hanging branches, marking them as "hazards" until they can be fixed, and fixing them promptly. A consistent record of inspection and repair shows a good faith attempt to provide a safe environment.

2 Actions of employees

Reduce this risk with preemployment screening and strong management. On-going training makes employees aware of liability issues, improves productivity, and creates a positive attitude toward safety.

3 Failure to deliver on an implied warranty

Advertising a community as "secure" can be interpreted as a warranty of safety. Other examples of implied warranties include "quiet environment" and "ample parking." Keep specific commitments to tenants within the terms of the lease. Let legal standards regulate more general commitments. For example, landlords are required to keep their properties in a safe and habitable condition.

4 Violation of residents' statutory rights

Residents with statutory right complaints are protected from retaliation, and stiff penalties can be imposed on the landlord. In communities with rent control ordinances, residents can strengthen their case against a landlord based on very small violations. Make sure you understand your current responsibilities under property management legislation.

5 Fair Housing violations

The government spends millions of dollars annually recruiting and training Fair Housing testers. These testers actively shop properties to identify discrimination against protected classes without waiting for specific complaints.

The 1968 Fair Housing Act prohibits discrimination in housing on the basis of race, color, religion, sex, and national origin. The act was amended in 1988, expanding the protected classes to include familial status and handicap. Individual jurisdictions may add to these classes but may not subtract from them. State and local statutes typically add marital status, sexual orientation, or other classifications at their discretion.

Among other scenarios, testers can cite property managers for discrimination if any staff member:

- Gives different counts of the number of units available
- Provides different lists of amenities
- Shows families with children first-floor units and childless couples units on higher floors.
- Tells applicants they wouldn't like a unit because of the stairs
- Assumes that families want to be close to the playground.
- Refuses to rent a studio to an obviously pregnant woman and her companion because the family will later exceed the occupancy criteria.
- Indicates that there are no vacancies without offering an application or waiting list option.

No other industry experiences such ongoing efforts to identify discrimination as the property management industry. Property managers and staff must constantly be trained and re-trained on Fair Housing.

PORTFOLIO PERFORMANCE

CHAPTER 15

10 WAYS TO IMPROVE YOUR MULTIFAMILY PORTFOLIO PERFORMANCE

FOLLOWING ARE 10 WAYS TO MAXIMIZE ROI AND CASH FLOW:

1 Eliminate small expenses, save big

Audit spending patterns. Does the site handyperson buy a gallon of paint at a time from the neighborhood hardware store? At many properties, making smaller purchases is easier for staff, but they may cost twice as much. Small items and petty cash purchases are often overlooked because individually they seem insignificant.

Buying paint and maintenance supplies in bulk and having items delivered can save staff time and supply costs. Ordering stamps on the Internet or by mail instead will leave your site manager in the office to greet potential residents. There are many similar money-saving examples.

2 Recover the costs to restore a unit to rentable condition

Most landlord–tenant statutes make the landlord responsible for normal "wear and tear" However, residents can cause damage in excess of this threshold. When they do, they can be held responsible if—and only if—management has maintained adequate documentation.

When a tenant moves in, prepare a checklist that describes the condition of the unit. Ensure the resident signs this, because it provides your legal "wear and tear" baseline. On notice to vacate, but before move-out, re-inspect the apartment with the resident present. Again, require the resident to sign a checklist.

After move-out, prepare a third checklist, including photographs of any significant damage or change from the findings of the pre-move-out inspection. Give the resident the market cost of each repair, and deduct the cost from the security deposit.

3 Do regular utility audits

Utilities are one of the largest expenses of a multifamily property. Energy costs have risen much faster than the overall rate of inflation. The good news is that utility companies are now encouraging lower consumption. Tap their knowledge and resources by requesting regular energy audits. You'll learn current methods such as refund and rebate programs to achieve cost savings.

4 Maximize staff time

Maximize your investment in on-site staff by assigning them to simple routine maintenance projects. Use contractors only for repairs requiring special licensing, unusual skill sets, or specialized tools and equipment.

5 Evict delinquent tenants

Every day that delinquent tenants stay means unrecoverable revenue. Use the legal process to remove them from your property as quickly as possible. If you do not move decisively, these tenants may try to justify their delinquency by bringing up grievances or pursuing legal action against you.

6 Make small repairs before they become big problems

Deferred maintenance devalues a property over the long term. A tube of caulking is a small expense compared to replacing an entire wall. The cost of putting off repairs is significant. A program of regular maintenance preserves the value of your investment.

7 Know the value of your property

A property valuation can save you thousands on property tax. Similar properties should be taxed similarly, but in many cases, they aren't. A property valuation can tell you whether your property is being over-taxed or not.

8 Know your insurance risks

Know your insurance policy, because exclusions can cost you thousands in uncovered losses. Find out what is and is not included before an unexpected loss occurs. While it is important to get competitive bids on insurance, you must first establish what you need to protect your asset.

9 Track your advertising dollars

Do you know where your traffic comes from? Ask prospects, "How did you hear about us?" With this information, you'll know what brings them to your door, as well as the features / benefits that cause them to lease. This will guide you in spending your advertising dollars.

10 Run the numbers, do the analysis

When markets are rising or falling rapidly, it's easy to lose track of your property's financial performance. Make a practice of running monthly and quarterly ratios on all of your reports. Based on the information, review your occupancy, rent, and cost targets and set new ones if necessary. This will help you keep your property's performance at the top of its market potential.

10 TIPS FOR EFFICIENT RISK MANAGEMENT

CHAPTER 16

Investing in multifamily property apartments carries inevitable risks. Risk can be reduced through solid teamwork by your attorney, accountant, financial planner, and property management staff.

FOLLOWING ARE 10 TIPS TO REDUCE YOUR EXPOSURE TO FINANCIAL LOSS:

1 Create a legal "firewall" between properties, employees, and your personal assets

Think of a pyramid of safety. First, do not co-mingle legal title to the property with your personal assets. Second, do not co-mingle legal title of multiple properties. Third, do not co-mingle the employee / employer relationships with either your personal assets or the property. This liability structure separates personal, property, and employee risk by placing a legal firewall between exposure to legal liability and assets.

2 Obtain resident waivers upfront to reduce exposures related to operating practices

Ask your attorney about including liability waivers with your lease package. Have residents sign liability waivers when they sign their leases. Consumers today expect to sign more than one document when they enter a major transaction, so this should not create a problem.

3 Deal proactively with mold exposure issues

Look for mold during unit turnovers and inspections, and get rid of it. Keep detailed move-in records with photographs. Give new residents tips on keeping mold away.

Deal with mold complaints as serious issues and document them.

4 Train all staff on the Federal Fair Housing Act

Every business requires constant training and professional development. In the case of property management, each staff meeting should include a discussion of some aspect of Fair Housing requirements.

The Department of Housing and Urban Development (HUD) regularly conducts audits designed to identify discrimination in housing. These audits are unannounced and random. Fines can be staggering.

Ensure that your entire staff receives Fair-Housing training. An offhand comment by any staff member can be used to demonstrate hostility toward any of the groups protected by the Fair Housing Act.

5 Schedule regular hazard inspections

Survey your property regularly for hazardous situations like uneven walkways and low-hanging branches. Document every problem when it occurs, put appropriate warning signs in place, and correct the condition as soon as possible.

6 Rigorously screen all prospective employees

You can be held liable for an employee's incompetence or criminality. Before hiring, examine the person's job history, personal references, and conduct a background search and drug / alcohol check. Seek the advice of an employment law specialist before you establish your pre-employment screening standards and release forms.

7 Prioritize health and safety-related repairs

Keep your property safe. Deal with broken locks, damaged stairs and walkways, internal and external lighting, gas and electrical problem, and hazardous material removal immediately.

8 Conduct periodic legal audits

Multifamily housing is regulated by constantly changing local, state and federal regulations. The only way to ensure that you are not following outdated regulations is to have your attorney conduct a regular legal audit.

Include key on-site staff members in the audit. Ask your attorney to review new and revised sections of your operations manual and make sure that you are following the most current Fair Housing and rent control regulations.

9 Audit vendor licensing and insurance

You are liable for any damage that vendors cause while working for you. Before you hire a contractor, ask for proof of licensure and insurance coverage. Require vendors to send you their license and insurance policy renewal certificates every year.

10 Have a plan for handling dissatisfied residents

A dissatisfied resident is a lawsuit waiting to happen. Respond promptly to complaints about sensitive issues and address them effectively. Develop a plan for handling specific types of complaints and apply it consistently.

CHAPTER 17

9 BENEFITS OF USING A PROFESSIONAL PROPERTY MANAGEMENT COMPANY

The right property management company can maximize efficiency and produce better results than owner management. Professional management companies have the knowledge and experience to avoid unnecessary litigation, reduce costs, find responsible tenants, and increase rental profits.

1 Legal expertise

Rental housing laws are constantly changing and are often difficult to navigate. Professional management companies are committed to keeping abreast with the most current rental property laws and know how those laws can affect rental properties.

2 Professional credentials

Professional property managers hold important credentials such as Certified Property Manager (CPM®) and Accredited Residential Manager (ARM®). An organization that holds the Accredited Management Organization (AMO®) credential has earned a designation of outstanding performance. In addition, most states require that property managers hold a real estate license or a property manager's license.

3 Screening procedures

Professional management companies have established tenant screening procedures and know how to distinguish good from bad tenants. They are also able to find replacement tenants quickly and responsibly.

4 Rent collection

Management companies have procedures in place to efficiently collect rent or pursue litigation with non-paying or late-paying tenants. They know how to avoid wasting time and money.

5 Resident relationships

Professional managers maintain fair and objective relationships with tenants. At the same time, they are friendly and customer-service oriented in their daily dealings with residents.

6 Vendor trust

Management companies have relationships of trust with vendors and know which contractors offer the best, most cost-efficient service. Where these relationships are long-standing, professional management companies often receive preferential pricing.

7 24 / 7 availability

Many professional management companies provide 24-hour maintenance service and availability. Managers can be reached 24 / 7 to address emergency repairs or other unexpected events.

8 Stress-free ownership

Because professional management companies can effectively handle the issues property owners assign to them, they can lighten the burden of responsibility and anxiety that accompanies property ownership.

9 Reduced costs, increased profits

Because professional management companies know how to make the most cost-effective choices without compromising quality, they can decrease operating costs and increase returns on the property.

Call
1-888-423-8855
For Freedom!

CHAPTER 18

10 POINT CHECKLIST FOR CHOOSING A PROPERTY MANAGEMENT COMPANY

Working with a professional property management company can relieve the stress and anxiety that accompany property ownership. A good firm will accommodate your preferences regarding your level of involvement in managing your property while ensuring that your investment is preserved.

FOLLOWING ARE 10 KEYS TO CHOOSING AND WORKING WITH A PROFESSIONAL PROPERTY MANAGEMENT COMPANY:

1 Alignment of interests

A management company must understand and accept your goals for your property. If your interests are aligned, the firm can put in place an appropriate game plan.

Your goals may include the following:

- I want to increase the value of this property over the next five years and trade it for a larger property.
- I need to use the cash flow from this property to cover shortfalls from other investments for the next couple of years.
- I need to diversify into more markets using the value of this property as the base.

Your management company should be able to develop reliable benchmarks and methods of reporting progress toward your goals.

2 Professionalism

Professional property management companies follow established procedures, ensuring that results are guaranteed and responses are consistent. At the property, staff wears uniforms that clearly identify them and respond rapidly and effectively to inquiries and emergencies. Their work ensures confidence.

3 Long-term commitment

Property management firms come and go. When evaluating a management company, ask about the firm's ownership structure, financial strength, and history. Determine whether property management feeds a core business such as real estate brokerage or development or is, in fact, the company's primary business focus.

4 Professional credentials

The easiest, most effective way to determine that a property management company hires qualified staff is to confirm that they are credentialed by major real estate trade associations such as the Institute of Real Estate Management, the National Apartment Association, and the National Association of Home Builders. These associations require rigorous education and testing and mandate high levels of experience for top-level certifications.

A property management firm staffed by Certified Property Managers (CPM®) and Accredited Residential Managers (ARM®) has hired professionals who are experienced, knowledgeable, and committed to ongoing training and development.

5 Timely reporting

Request timely exception reporting. A narrative overview from your management company that confirms exceptions should appear at the top of the report. This eliminates surprises and makes it easier to address problems while they are easily solvable.

6 Single point of contact

Your property management company should provide you with a single point of contact and make that person easily available to you 24/7. Your contact should have the authority to move quickly through the internal chain of command and get the answers you need immediately. A direct line of communication is the key to minimizing expense and improving revenues.

7 Easily-understood budgets

Budgets should include critical items, goals, and key benchmarks translated into relevant numbers. Whether or not targets are being met should be obvious at first glance.

8 Experience with complex capital structures

Your property management company should have broad, deep experience in working with sophisticated transactions and structures. A strong management team understands complex objectives and offers competitive strategies that enable you to reach your goals.

9 Matching perspectives

Your property management firm's perspective should match your own. Some firms work best for institutional owners. Others work best on new developments, low-income properties, or family-owned portfolios. When seeking a property management firm, ask about its experience with various types of ownership. Find out whether it tailors its approach to meet your goals or whether you must buy a packaged service that may compromise them.

10 Good working relationships

Because you will spend a lot of time with your property management team, find a group with whom you enjoy working.

APPENDIX

Suggested Resource Associations

- IREM.org
- CAA.org
- BOMA.org
- DRE.CA.gov

Also check out:

- San Francisco Rent Board @ www.sfgov.org/site/rentboard
- National Apartment Association @ www.naahq.org
- Department of Justice @ www.usdoj.gov
- California Law Website @ www.leginfo.ca.gov
- Department of Fair Employment & Housing @ www.dfeh.ca.gov
- National MultiHousing Council @ www.nmhc.org
- California Department of Housing & Community Development @ www.hcd.ca.gov
- California Housing Finance Agency @ www.calhfa.ca.gov
- National Affordable Housing Management Association @ www.nahma.org
- National Center for Housing Management @ www.nchm.org
- Tenant Screening with ChoicePoint @ www.choicepoint.com
- Tenant Screening with ScreeningOne @ www.screeningone.com

AUTHORS

Robert W. Klag, CPA
Chief Executive Officer

Robert Klag brings more than 25 years of management experience and strong operational leadership to Westlake. Prior to joining the company in 2003, he headed financial operations at PrimeSight, a national healthcare provider, and led a team that successfully enrolled 200,000 subscribers in two years. Mr. Klag has also been senior vice president of finance and treasurer at National Insurance Group where he helped build the company into a national provider of specialized risk management and outsourced service products.

Earlier in his career, he was with KPMG LLP and General Electric. As Administration Manager for General Electric's Canadian Mineral Operations, he managed real property holdings, reducing fixed operating costs by more than $1 million per year.

Mr. Klag holds a B.S. in economics at the University of California Riverside and an M.B.A. from the University of California Berkeley. Mr. Klag is a certified public accountant, and a certified management accountant. He is a member of the California Association of Certified Public Accountants, the American Institute of Certified Public Accountants, and the Institute of Certified Management Accountants.

Gemma G. Lim
Director of Business Development

Gemma Lim joined Westlake in 2002. She brings more than 12 years of experience in advertising, branding, market research, and marketing strategy to Westlake's corporate marketing and business development activities. Prior to Westlake, Ms. Lim was an account manager at an international HR consulting firm and generated 45% of the firm's revenues. She also managed marketing projects at Unilever Bestfoods and DuPont Inc. where she successfully developed and implemented high impact, low budget marketing promotions.

Earlier in her career, Ms. Lim was a treasury manager for J.G Summit Holdings Inc, a $2.4 billion global conglomerate with major real estate holdings. In this role, she established treasury systems in two key cities in China, approved all financial transaction, and monitored land values for the company's commercial property investments.

Ms. Lim holds a B.S. in management from Ateneo de Manila University and an M.B.A from Fordham University in New York. A CRE license candidate, she is fluent in 3 languages. She is a member of Building Owners and Managers Association (BOMA), the International Council of Shopping Centers (ICSC), and various Chambers of Commerce.

Steven M. McDonald, CPM®
Vice President & General Manager, Residential Properties

Since joining Westlake in 2004, Steven McDonald has develope[d] and implemented policy and procedure improvements, increas[-]ing occupancy rates as well as maximizing top-line revenues and net operating income. Prior to joining Westlake, Mr. McDonald had more than 20 years of experience directing federal and state subsidized housing programs and in managing conventional market-driven rental properties. Mr. McDonald has been involved with a number of California non-profit organizations including First Community Housing, Housing for Independent People (HIP), Community Housing Developers (CHD), Soledad Local Development Co. (SLDC), and Catholic Charities.

Mr. McDonald holds Housing Credit Certified Professional (HCCP), Certified Occupancy Specialist (COS), and National Compliance Professional (NCP) certifications. He is a graduate of San Jose State University, has a California real estate license, and is a Certified Property Manager (CPM®) through the Institute of Real Estate Management. Mr. McDonald serves on the Board of IREM-SF as vice president of membership.

M. Gary Wong
President, Westlake Development Partners and Westlake Realty Advisors

Mr. Wong joined Westlake in 2002 and has served as CFO, COO, and president of the Chang Family Office. His current responsibilities include overseeing Westlake's real estate portfolio and developing the company's land holding. Mr. Wong has extensive experience in finance and the capital markets, serving as senior vice president for corporate finance at Wedbush Morgan Securities for 15 years and as a vice president at the Bank of America for six years.

Mr. Wong is a member of the Policy Advisory Board for the Fisher Center for Real Estate and Urban Economics, the Urban Land Institute, Building Owners and Managers Association (BOMA), and the International Council of Shopping Centers. He has served on the corporate board and as treasurer of the United Way of Los Angeles and is a Block Leader for the City of Cupertino. He holds a B.A. and an M.B.A. from the University of California, Berkeley.

WRITE YOUR BOOK

Create thought leadership for your company! Books deliver instant credibility to an author. Having an MBA or PhD is great. However, putting the word "author" in front of your name is powerful. You are no longer Michael Green, you are "Author Michael Green." Books give you a platform to stand on and will help you demonstrate your thought leadership and create leads. Books are more powerful than white papers and end up on the bookshelf of your prospective clients. Your knowledge and information are absolutely the best things you can share with others.

They help you to:

- Demonstrate your thought leadership
- Generate leads

Books deliver increased revenue, particularly indirect revenue

- A typical consultant will make 3x in indirect revenue for every dollar they make on book sales

Books are better than a business card. They are:

- More powerful than white papers
- An item that makes it to the bookshelf vs. the circular file
- Better to give away at a conference than the latest tschochke

Why wait to write your book? Check out some of the other companies that have built credibility through writing a book and publishing with Happy About.

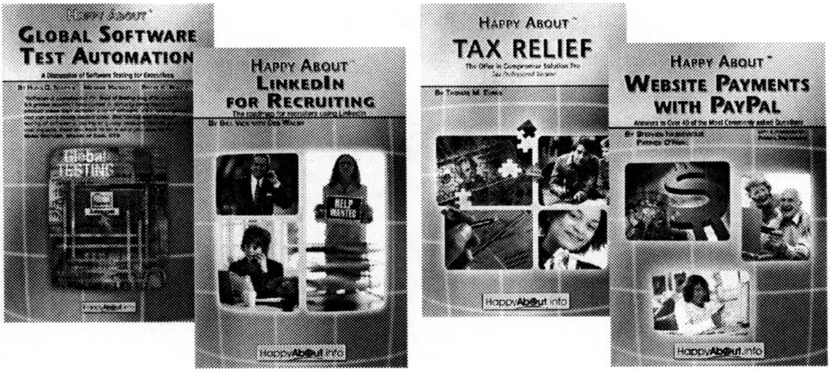

Contact Happy About at 408-257-3000 or go to
http://happyabout.info

A MESSAGE FROM HAPPY ABOUT®

Thank you for your purchase of this Happy About® book. It is available online at http://HappyAbout.info/apartment-management.php or at other online and physical bookstores.

- Please contact us for quantity discounts at: sales@happyabout.info.
- If you want to be informed by e-mail of upcoming Happy About® books, please e-mail: bookupdate@happyabout.info.
- If you want to contribute to upcoming Happy About® books, please go to http://happyabout.info/contribute/

Happy About is interested in you if you are an author who would like to submit a non-fiction book proposal. Please contact us by e-mail: editorial@happyabout.info or phone (1-408-257-3000).

Other Happy About books available include:

Happy About Online Networking
http://happyabout.info/onlinenetworking.php

Memoirs of the Money Lady
http://happyabout.info/memoirs-money-lady.php

30 Day BootCamp: Your Ultimate Life Makeover
http://happyabout.info/30daybootcamp/life-makeover.php

Business Rule Revolution
http://happyabout.info/business-rule-revolution.php

Happy About Global Software Test Automation:
http://happyabout.info/globalswtestautomation.php

Happy About Joint Venturing:
http://happyabout.info/jointventuring.php

Happy About LinkedIn for Recruiting:
http://happyabout.info/linkedin4recruiting.php

Happy About Website Payments with PayPal
http://happyabout.info/paypal.php

Happy About Outsourcing
http://happyabout.info/outsourcing.php

Happy About Knowing What to Expect in 2006
http://happyabout.info/economy.php

ABOUT WESTLAKE REALTY GROUP, INC.

Headquartered in the San Francisco Bay Area, Westlake Realty Group brings more than 30 years of experience to managing multifamily residential units, affordable housing, retirement communities, office buildings, mixed-use properties, and shopping centers in Arizona, California, Nevada, New Mexico, Oregon, and Washington.

We are successful at what we do because we offer genuine value to the owners and tenants of the properties we manage. We are well known in the industry for spending more time on activities that increase property values and enhance the tenant experience rather than on non-value-producing paperwork.

Westlake combines expert property stewardship with technology to reduce costs, increase ROI, and preserve asset value. Our use of secure electronic filing systems, imaging, desktop banking, and wireless communication devices enables us to operate without boundaries, providing the same excellent level of service to our clients whether from our offices or on the road. Westlake management teams are both proactive and highly responsive as situations demand, delivering what property owners require, when they require it. Our goal is to "pay our way" through ongoing cost savings.

Westlake is committed to continuous improvement not only of the technology we use but also in the education of our staff. Our executive team holds the most advanced certifications awarded by the industry and represents more than 300 years of combined experience. We also provide significant incentives for our property managers and other employees to expand their skills, because we believe training is an investment that pays off for owners, tenants, and our company.

In everything we do, Westlake stays focused on flexibility, productivity, efficiency, and control, bringing together the critical resources necessary for success.

Westlake Realty Group, Inc.
Corporate Office
520 South El Camino Real, 9th Floor
San Mateo, California, 94402 USA
TEL: 1-650-579-1010
TOLL FREE: 1.888.423.8855
FAX: 1-650-340-8252
www.westlake-realty.com

Real People. Real Solutions. Real Time™

Additional Praise for 'Happy About Apartment Management'

"This book provides a head start for apartment owners who want to learn from 30 years of experience."
Kyle R. Klopfer, CPA - Klopfer & Associates

"This is an easy to read, practical and insightful guide for property owners and managers and those who are planning to get into the business. It will quickly become an essential reference book for the industry.
— I strongly recommend it."
Stephen A. Cowan, Partner, DLA Piper

"Westlake Realty Group's vast experience in property management and their success speak for itself. Any owner/manager of an apartment complex would be wise to follow the advice and wisdom in 'Happy About Apartment Management' from these successful real estate professionals."
Gino Blefari, Founder, President and CEO
Intero Real Estate Services

"It is clear why Westlake Realty Group is so successful, they pay attention to every detail and have created apartment communities that are more than just lodging, but create a quality lifestyle.
— Great advice from experts!"
Kevin F. Kilty, Vice President JD, ARM
UnionBanc Insurance Services, Inc.

"I wish I had read the 9 Keys to Credit Screening before renting my property"
Amalia Gaiotto, Rental Property Owner